SAM STEINER

Sam Steiner is a playwright and screenwriter who hails from Manchester. His plays include *Lemons Lemons Lemons Lemons Lemons* (Walrus Theatre, Edinburgh Festival Fringe for three sold-out runs, 2015); *Kanye the First* (HighTide, 2017); *A Table Tennis Play* (Walrus Theatre, Edinburgh Festival Fringe, 2019); *You Stupid Darkness!* (Paines Plough & Theatre Royal Plymouth, 2019 and Southwark Playhouse, 2020). He also has new commissions with the Almeida Theatre and Francesca Moody. To date, *Lemons Lemons Lemons Lemons Lemons*, which is frequently studied on post-graduate level courses, has been performed all over the world in over a dozen languages.

Sam's current feature slate includes *Morning*, which Justin Kurzel is directing. Laura Dern, Benedict Cumberbatch and Noah Jupe will star, with Cumberbatch's Sunnymarch producing. He has two films currently in production: *Fingernails*, which Christos Nikou (*Apples*) is directing for Apple, starring Jessie Buckley and Riz Ahmed, and *Rich Flu*, which Galder Gaztelu-Urrutia (*The Platform*) is directing, starring Mary-Elizabeth Winstead. He is also working on *Banquet*, an original horror with David Yates producing, and original feature drama *The Endling*, with Tessa Ross and Sarah Esberg producing.

Sam Steiner

LEMONS LEMONS LEMONS LEMONS LEMONS

NICK HERN BOOKS

London

www.nickhernbooks.co.uk

A Nick Hern Book

Lemons Lemons Lemons Lemons Lemons first published in Great Britain in 2015 as a paperback original by Nick Hern Books Limited, The Glasshouse, 49a Goldhawk Road, London W12 8QP

Reprinted in this new edition in 2023

Lemons Lemons Lemons Lemons Lemons copyright © 2015, 2023 Sam Steiner

Sam Steiner has asserted his moral right to be identified as the author of this work

Cover image: Aidan Turner and Jenna Coleman in the 2023 revival, photograph by Jason Bell, artwork by Feast Creative

Designed and typeset by Nick Hern Books, London
Printed in Great Britain by Mimeo Ltd, Huntingdon, Cambridgeshire PE29 6XX

A CIP catalogue record for this book is available from the British Library

ISBN   978 1 83904 145 7

On Changes
Sam Steiner

It's hard for me not to be sentimental about this play.

This version of *Lemons Lemons Lemons Lemons Lemons* was written for Josie Rourke's 2023 revival of the play at the Harold Pinter Theatre. Revisiting and revising the play for a new context, eight very formative years after it was first written, has been a strange, daunting and reflective experience.

Returning to the text, there are jokes I cringe at; passages I find a bit on the nose; beats that feel unclear, arguments unbalanced. But there's a spirit to the thing that belongs to the person I was when I wrote it, the context it was written in and the people I wrote it for and with. And it's that spirit that, I think, has given the play what life it's had since then.

The job of this new pass has been, in part, to use whatever skill, craft and, well, life, I've amassed in the intervening time to amplify and clarify that spirit. Without altering it. I've tried to listen to the play. Go where it wants to go. Not to impose my current tastes upon it. Not to chase any cultural, social or political resonances that the play may have with the happenings of the last few years. To write, essentially, in a big citrusy vacuum.

But how much that's actually possible, I don't know. I think, probably, the stuff of life gets in.

The best moments of this rewrite, the most purely pleasurable, were those when I felt I'd unearthed something true about the characters or the story that I hadn't quite realised before. There's a new stage direction halfway through this version that reads '*They look at each other, panting, full of adrenalin*'. This feels, to me, both true of that particular moment for Oliver and Bernadette and, amusingly, of my experience writing it. I was short of breath, hocked up on adrenalin, realising that something was happening between these two people at this moment that I'd never understood previously. What a special thing – to have the chance to refind a piece of work you thought you'd seen every corner of.

I couldn't say if this version is 'better'. It feels a little bigger to me, a little *fuller*, for what that's worth. Josie describes these changes as a 'maturing' of the play. That's certainly true of the characters, who now feel more thirties than twenties, and the relationship, which feels longer and (therefore?) perhaps more painful when it breaks down. If you're thinking of putting this play on I'd probably encourage you to read both versions and choose whichever one feels right to you.

By strange coincidence, today is the eighth anniversary of the play's first-ever performance. I was twenty-one. The West End production will begin previews two days after my thirtieth birthday. Years later, it's still revealing itself to me. I hope to keep learning from it. And I hope it's a fun read.

7 January 2023

Lemons Lemons Lemons Lemons Lemons premiered at the Warwick Arts Centre in January 2015 before heading to the National Student Drama Festival in March, where it won three awards, including judges' commendations for writing and direction. The production visited the Latitude Festival in July before a sell-out run at Zoo Southside at the Edinburgh Festival Fringe, and transferred to Camden People's Theatre on 24 November 2015. The cast was as follows:

OLIVER	Euan Kitson
BERNADETTE	Beth Holmes
Director	Ed Madden

Lemons Lemons Lemons Lemons Lemons was revived on 31 January 2023 at the Harold Pinter Theatre, London (previews from 18 January), produced by Wessex Grove, Gavin Kalin Productions and Francesca Moody Productions. The cast was as follows:

BERNADETTE	Jenna Coleman
OLIVER	Aidan Turner
UNDERSTUDY BERNADETTE	Katie Buchholz
UNDERSTUDY OLIVER	David Buttle

Director	Josie Rourke
Designer	Robert Jones
Lighting Designer	Aideen Malone
Sound Designer	George Dennis
Movement Director	Annie-Lunnette Deakin-Foster
Casting	Jim Carnahan CSA & Alexandre Bleau CSA
Associate Director	Sean Linnen
Associate Costume Designer	Kinnetia Isidore
Associate Sound Designer	Sam Clarkson for Sound Quiet Time
Props Supervisor	Lisa Buckley
Voice Coach	Nick Trumble
Assistant Director	Caroline Yu
Assistant Lighting Designer	Jessica Brigham

Thanks

To our Edinburgh team and everyone along the way: Josie Davies, Oscar Owen, Antonia Salib, Hattie Collins, Shakira, George Attwell Gerhards, Ellice Stevens, Sarah Georgeson, Alexandra Spencer-Jones, everyone at NSDF, Matt Burman, and Laura Elliot.

To Rebecca Jane Webster, Harry Mallon, Rebecca Myers, Anna Canlan-Shaw, Jiggy Steiner and Josh Steiner for their love, support and inspiration.

To Beth Holmes and Euan Kitson, whose play this really is.

To Ed Madden, who gave me the idea. And most other things.

S.S.
2015

Some More Thanks

To Josie Rourke for bringing this play into the light with piercing intelligence, sensitivity, humour and a breathtaking knack for an analogy.

To Jenna Coleman and Aidan Turner for throwing themselves into these characters with such depth of thought, tenderness and wit.

To our alarmingly inspiring creative team for their artistry, imagination and sense of scale. Working with you all has changed my understanding of what this play can be.

To Emily Vaughan-Barratt, Francesca Moody, Benjamin Lowy, Gavin Kalin and everyone at Wessex Grove for making it happen.

To my agents Marnie Podos, John MacGregor, Jon Cassir, Paige Holtzman and Wilhelmina Ross for always being in my corner.

To Jess Bray for fixing the play for me during an everlasting series of Zoom calls just after she'd got back from a run.

To Charlotte, for all her support, her time and her infectious optimism when mine was lacking.

S.S.
2023

For my mum and dad

Characters

BERNADETTE
OLIVER

Note on Text

A forward slash (/) indicates interrupted speech.

They speak slowly and quietly.

OLIVER. Thirty-four.

BERNADETTE. Twenty-one.

> *Pause.*

> Day?

OLIVER. Yeah. Yours?

BERNADETTE. Yeah. Tuesday happened again.

OLIVER. Sorry.

BERNADETTE. Well, sorf.

OLIVER. Fuck it.

> *Pause.*

> Talk?

BERNADETTE. Thirteen. You talk.

OLIVER. About?

> BERNADETTE *shrugs*.

> Bernadette.

BERNADETTE. I know.

OLIVER. I can't know you in one hundred forty.

> *Pause.*

BERNADETTE. Try.

                              *

OLIVER. We need to stop meeting here. It's all a bit morbid.

BERNADETTE. Well, it's the only place that I know that you know.

OLIVER. You've never asked where else I know.

BERNADETTE. Well, maybe I just like revisiting the graves of dead cats. Maybe I'm just that kind of girl.

OLIVER. Maybe we should talk about other places we could meet.

Pause.

I told my friend Eliot / about you

BERNADETTE. Eliot's the one that played trumpet on / your latest

OLIVER. Yeah / and

BERNADETTE. The one who's really pro-word limit.

OLIVER. Yeah. Fascist fuck. Anyway I told him that I'd met a… person… and that she was you, you know, that her name was Bernadette and that she had… like I described you to him, your features and everything.

BERNADETTE. Would kill to overhear this conversation.

OLIVER. That you're a lawyer / and stuff

BERNADETTE. Training.

OLIVER. And then he asked me where we met.

BERNADETTE. You didn't tell / him that

OLIVER. That we met at a funeral for a cat named Dennis? No.

BERNADETTE. Steph was heartbroken and the service was very powerful.

OLIVER. Or that we…

BERNADETTE. Continued to meet at the pet cemetery for…

OLIVER. No.

BERNADETTE. So you haven't actually told him…

OLIVER. No. I told him we met at a book club.

BERNADETTE *raises her eyebrows*.

I'd also been lying about having a book club.

BERNADETTE *grins. Pause.*

I think we should talk about other places that we could meet. Y'know like sausage factories. Or abattoirs.

BERNADETTE. Yeah. We should. We should. It's just…

OLIVER. Yep.

BERNADETTE. That I don't really know you outside the pet cemetery, Oliver. I don't know you when you're around other people really.

OLIVER. Only the carcasses of dead animals.

BERNADETTE. Yeah.

OLIVER. Right.

BERNADETTE. And what if you're like a different guy when you're not around the…

OLIVER. The… yeah.

BERNADETTE. Yeah.

OLIVER. I think I'm pretty much the same.

BERNADETTE. Yeah obviously / you are but…

OLIVER. If a little less on edge.

BERNADETTE. No obviously you're the same. But what, okay, what if, when there are more people around and when there are smells and billboards and cinemas and like fast-food restaurants and rock music and people on the street selling burgers…

OLIVER. Do you live in like, a child's drawing of a city?

BERNADETTE. And parents and friends and *exes*.

OLIVER. Right.

BERNADETTE. Sorry.

OLIVER. Do you not want to be seen with…

BERNADETTE. No! It's not.

OLIVER. Okay?

BERNADETTE. No no no no it's just all… out there you know… it's ahhhhhhhhhhhhhhh.

Pause.

OLIVER. 'Ahhhhh'?

Pause.

I don't really eat many burgers and I'm quite good at shutting out street sellers. Like shutting them down. Downtown.

BERNADETTE. Here, it's just this. It's just… this.

OLIVER. You're scared.

BERNADETTE (*laughing*). I'm scared.

OLIVER. Of smells and cinemas and rock music.

BERNADETTE. Of things getting / in the

OLIVER. Yeah.

Pause.

Well, me too.

Scared, I mean.

Beat.

BERNADETTE. Okay.

OLIVER. Okay?

BERNADETTE. Okay.

I was just checking.

*

OLIVER *is crouched on the floor.* BERNADETTE *stands, looking down at him sceptically.* OLIVER *taps out: Dot dash dash dot. Pause. Dot dash dot. Pause. Dot dash. Pause. Dash dot dash dot. Pause. Dash. Pause. Dot dot. Pause. Dot dot dot. Pause. Dot.*

BERNADETTE *looks weary and motions as if to say 'I have no idea what you just said.'*

OLIVER. Fuck.

*

BERNADETTE. Hi.

OLIVER. Hi. You look nice. High heels.

BERNADETTE. Yeah, you didn't tell me where we were going... so I dressed nice. Where are we going?

OLIVER. We're going zorbing.

BERNADETTE. What?

OLIVER. We're going for sushi.

*

They are playing Articulate.

OLIVER. Ready?

BERNADETTE. Yep. Ready.

OLIVER. Okay right, right. Band. They're a band. They were big in the eighties. Absolutely awful, music-wise. Not damp damp damp.

BERNADETTE. Wet Wet Wet.

OLIVER. Yep. Okay so these are like, right, like peninsulas but they've got water all the way round.

BERNADETTE. Islands.

OLIVER. Yep but they're... chaste.

BERNADETTE. They're *chaste*?

OLIVER. They've never had sex.

BERNADETTE. Virgin Islands.

*

OLIVER. Nineteen.

BERNADETTE. Two. Hungry?

OLIVER *nods*.

OLIVER. Want?

BERNADETTE. Lamb –

OLIVER. Lamb what?

BERNADETTE *looks at him helplessly*.

Zero?

BERNADETTE *nods*.

Shepherd's pie?

BERNADETTE *pulls a disgusted expression*.

Stew?

BERNADETTE *shakes her head*.

Rogan josh?

BERNADETTE *shakes her head and begins to mime 'kebabs'*.

Lollipop.

Pause. BERNADETTE *sighs and relaxes her hands down into a handlebars-like position*.

Hang-glider?

*

OLIVER. Morning.

BERNADETTE. Morning.

OLIVER. Hi.

BERNADETTE *smiles*.

BERNADETTE. Hi.

OLIVER. You talk in your sleep.

BERNADETTE. What did I say?

OLIVER. It was pretty hard to tell. Something about Batman stealing your pens. Think it was Batman. Could've been a 'bad man'.

Pause.

BERNADETTE. It was a bad man.

*

BERNADETTE. Hi.

OLIVER. Hi.

BERNADETTE. I like coming home to you.

*

OLIVER. Sixteen.

BERNADETTE. Twenty-four.

OLIVER. What do?

BERNADETTE. Bed?

OLIVER. Half seven.

BERNADETTE *nods*.

Tired?

BERNADETTE *nods*.

BERNADETTE. You?

OLIVER *nods*.

You're always tired.

Pause.

Obsessing over count.

OLIVER. Badly today.

BERNADETTE. Too much going on.

*

BERNADETTE. When was the last time you saw her?

OLIVER. I see her every now and then. We go on those marches. Against the Hush Law.

BERNADETTE. Bill.

OLIVER. Bill.

BERNADETTE. She's the one that's really into it?

OLIVER. Yeah. She almost ran against them in Basildon.

BERNADETTE. As an independent?

OLIVER. Yep.

BERNADETTE. Why Basildon?

OLIVER. She thought there was a diverse voter base or something. Lots of undecideds.

BERNADETTE. But you're... you're into it too. The marches.

OLIVER. Yeah.

BERNADETTE. Why did you break up?

OLIVER. It was just time.

BERNADETTE. Why was it time?

OLIVER. I don't know, Bernadette. A whole host of reasons.

BERNADETTE. And you see her every now and then. For the –

OLIVER. Yeah.

BERNADETTE. Well then, I want to see her every now and then. If she's your 'anti-establishment buddy' then I want her to be my like normal buddy.

OLIVER. You could come to the meetings?

BERNADETTE (*uncertainly*). Yeah.

OLIVER. Yeah?

BERNADETTE. Yeah – no – I could. I always feel a bit... stupid / at those

OLIVER. What? You're like the smartest / person I know.

BERNADETTE. But it's different, it's... No, I'll come, I will! If you want me to?

OLIVER....Sure.

Beat.

BERNADETTE. What do what's-her-name

OLIVER. Julie.

BERNADETTE. Julie. What do Julie's parents do?

OLIVER. Uh... they're paediatricians. Why?

BERNADETTE. Nothing. Just... curious.

OLIVER. You knew what her name was.

BERNADETTE. I did yep.

Beat.

OLIVER. What's going on?

BERNADETTE. I want you to tell me all your things.

OLIVER. What?

BERNADETTE. All of your and... uh – (*Pretends to have forgotten it again.*)

OLIVER. Fuck off.

BERNADETTE. All of you and Julie's things.

OLIVER. Things?

BERNADETTE. Yeah. Oliver, every couple has their own kind of little... language. Behaviours.

OLIVER. Right.

BERNADETTE. Like a dialect.

OLIVER. Like Canadian French.

BERNADETTE. Kind of like Canadian French but small-scale I guess.

OLIVER. Like if there were only two people in Canada and they both used to be French.

BERNADETTE. Yeah. Like your own set of in-jokes and pet names and little ways of phrasing things that just develop. And I know that I've recycled them before. And I don't want that to… Like I'll be talking in one guy's, an ex's, language and making our jokes and saying things in ways that we came up with together and then I'll turn around and it'll be this completely different, new man in front of me and he doesn't get… he thinks I've got this really weird way of talking and *being* that isn't funny or endearing or sexy, it's just weird.

OLIVER. So he didn't understand what you were…

BERNADETTE. No, no. He understood. We were speaking in English. It was just as if English had been… okay imagine you've got a cheese grater. One of those cheese graters with the four different sides that grates the four different types of cheese gratings. It's like each one of those sides is a different relationship and while I was with Stuart I was grating my cheese on one side of the grater and the cheese came out in a really weird shape that we'd, I dunno, designed together. Then when I was with Clint I kept grating my cheese on the same weird side out of habit and Clint would lift up the grater, look at the grated cheese and be like 'what the fuck?' Like 'this isn't the mature cheddar that I know and love.'

OLIVER. Cheese is language.

BERNADETTE. Yeah. But more than that. He was looking at me like: who's this strange woman and what's she doing in my house?

Like that version of me was so foreign to him. Like it didn't fit.

Beat.

OLIVER. You went out with a Clint?

BERNADETTE. Yep. For like four years. Weird to think of now.

OLIVER. Four years!?

BERNADETTE. He was actually lactose intolerant. Not metaphorically... he genuinely struggled with dairy.

OLIVER. Well I'm really good with dairy. Like I have a very capable stomach.

BERNADETTE. I want you to tell me all of your things so that I never have to lift the grater up and find someone else's cheese in our kitchen.

OLIVER. Metaphorically...?

BERNADETTE. Yeah.

OLIVER. Right.

BERNADETTE. Oliver, please.

Pause.

OLIVER. Okay. Errrrm. Well, I can't remember most of them. But we... okay so we started calling each other... babycakes.

BERNADETTE. Babycakes?

OLIVER. It started off ironically. But by the end it felt almost natural. Don't look at me.

BERNADETTE. Babycakes?

OLIVER. This is horrible.

BERNADETTE. I just want all the stuff we say to each other to be stuff that we haven't said a million times before. Or at least like we're saying it in a new way that is just... I know this is ridiculous.

OLIVER. It is ridiculous.

BERNADETTE. I'm sorry.

OLIVER. You're being neurotic.

BERNADETTE. I'm not neurotic.

OLIVER. I know but you're being it.

BERNADETTE. I know.

OLIVER. I love you.

Silence.

BERNADETTE. Have you said that before?

OLIVER. Yeah.

BERNADETTE. To other people?

OLIVER. Yeah.

BERNADETTE. Me too.

Pause.

Still sounds pretty good, I guess.

*

OLIVER. Can't wait to see you. I love you.

*

BERNADETTE. Happy birthday! I love you.

*

OLIVER. Merry Christmas! I love you.

*

BERNADETTE. Break a leg, I love you.

*

OLIVER. Listen, just listen, I love you. Why wouldn't they?

*

BERNADETTE. Yeah, of course I love you. I'm sorry.

*

OLIVER. Yeah, you sign the lease now, I'll sign it when I get there. Yeah, I love you.

*

BERNADETTE. Hey, it's just one person's opinion. Promise me you won't take it too personally. I love you.

*

OLIVER. I knew you'd get it! You're the perfect fucking candidate! Okay I'm booking a table somewhere. Love you.

*

BERNADETTE. Yeah, love you. It's saying I need your National Insurance number? Did you send that me?

*

OLIVER. And it's like: I know that I, like, love you. I know that to be true. So why do I need some piece of paper...?

*

BERNADETTE. I love you, okay? I love you. But I need to focus right now. I've left the dishes.

*

OLIVER. I love you.

*

BERNADETTE. I love you.

*

OLIVER. Ninety-eight.

BERNADETTE. Thirteen. Good luck. Got your speech?

OLIVER *nods*.

Lovou.

OLIVER *nods*.

BERNADETTE. Lovou.

OLIVER. Lovou.

*

OLIVER. I saw Julie today.

BERNADETTE. Oh yeah? What do you want for dinner?

OLIVER. I don't mind.

BERNADETTE. Shall we get a takeaway?

OLIVER. Er yeah could do.

BERNADETTE. It's been one of those days.

OLIVER. Julie's dyed her hair red.

BERNADETTE. She did it?

OLIVER. Yep.

BERNADETTE. She told me she was thinking about it.

OLIVER. It looks awful.

BERNADETTE. Yeah I did a box when I was seventeen. Came out pink.

OLIVER. Oh she didn't do a box. Went to some place her mum swears by. Cost like two hundred quid.

BERNADETTE. Oh right wow.

OLIVER. So I had to pretend to like it.

BERNADETTE. I bet she looks great.

OLIVER. You're deeply mistaken.

BERNADETTE. I'm gonna order. Eliot called by the way.

OLIVER. I'm ignoring him. Can't take all those posts.

Pause.

But I was talking to Julie about the stuff I've been doing recently, playing with texture and instrumentation and stuff. Polyphony. And she was saying she knows this lyricist who's pretty much the next big / thing. And she...

BERNADETTE. You know when I was little I didn't think songs had words in them.

OLIVER. Bernadette, I was right in the middle of a story.

BERNADETTE. Sorry. Carry on.

OLIVER. I hate it when you do that.

BERNADETTE. I was enjoying it. Carry on.

OLIVER. I can literally see you drifting / off

BERNADETTE. I was listening. Julie's clever and rich.

OLIVER. There's always this moment with you when something I say makes you go 'oh yeah, that sounds a lot like my life' and / then you're off thinking about...

BERNADETTE. That's unfair. / You're being really unfair now.

OLIVER. You used to think songs didn't have words in them?

BERNADETTE. Yeah.

OLIVER. That's stupid.

BERNADETTE. I was little.

OLIVER. So what... What did you think they sang?

Pause.

BERNADETTE. Vowel sounds. Like kind of improvised vowel sounds in tune with the, I dunno, the rhythm. Like:

She sings a vowel-sound melody.

OLIVER. But you could... you knew / words.

BERNADETTE. Oh yeah I knew about words. That there were words. And I was speaking them by then, I was speaking. I just didn't know they were in...

OLIVER. Songs.

Pause.

Right.

BERNADETTE. You okay?

OLIVER. Yeah.

BERNADETTE. You're a bit serious today.

OLIVER. Sorry.

BERNADETTE. I'm sorry for interrupting you.

OLIVER. Sorry if I've been serious.

BERNADETTE. Where did you see posh Julie?

OLIVER. What?

BERNADETTE. Julie. Where did you see her?

OLIVER. Oh. The supermarket. She was buying falafel.

*

BERNADETTE. Thirty-six.

OLIVER. Six.

Long pause.

I'm sorry.

BERNADETTE. Tough day?

Pause.

OLIVER. Tough day.

BERNADETTE. Mine fine. Settled the Wilson case.

Pause.

OLIVER. I'm glad.

BERNADETTE. Zero?

OLIVER *nods*.

Joint custody. David gets weekends. Good they compromised.

Pause.

OLIVER *nods*.

*

OLIVER. So?

BERNADETTE. I really love it.

OLIVER. You do?

BERNADETTE. I do.

OLIVER. You like the flutes? And the little...

He hums a fanfare.

BERNADETTE. I do. I really love it.

OLIVER. Okay.

BERNADETTE. I've gotta go over some stuff.

OLIVER. When does the trial start?

BERNADETTE. Tomorrow.

OLIVER. First big trial.

BERNADETTE. First big trial.

OLIVER. I hate words like really.

BERNADETTE. What?

OLIVER. I really love it. You said: I really love it.

BERNADETTE. Okay...

OLIVER. Qualifiers.

BERNADETTE. Qualifiers?

OLIVER. I really love it. If you say: I love it, that's like wow what a nice compliment, she loves what I do. I really love it is like saying: Please believe that I like this thing. Believe it, believe it. Right, now let's just talk about my problems.

BERNADETTE. Whoa. That is really not. That is / not.

OLIVER. The only time anyone has ever meant the word 'really' is when Eva Cassidy sings it in 'Over the Rainbow'.

BERNADETTE. Oliver.

OLIVER. She goes: Reeeeeaaally.

BERNADETTE. Oliver.

OLIVER. Reeeeeeeaaallly. And it's like you can see everything she's dreamt of materialising in front of / her eyes.

BERNADETTE. You're insecure.

OLIVER. No, I'm not.

BERNADETTE. You're insecure about being insecure.

Pause.

OLIVER. No, I'm not.

BERNADETTE. I love your stuff. Okay?

OLIVER. Yeah.

BERNADETTE. Okay?

OLIVER. Yeah. With this stuff... I am just a bit...

BERNADETTE. Yeah. Listen I've gotta look over some stuff.

Pause.

OLIVER. I never thought I'd go out with a lawyer.

BERNADETTE. Well I always thought I'd be one so...

OLIVER. I know.

BERNADETTE. Sorry I can't live to your standards.

OLIVER. That is really not what I'm saying.

Pause.

That's not what I said.

Pause.

BERNADETTE. Can we talk about this later?

OLIVER. Sure.

Silence.

*

OLIVER. Look, I need to get this done. Let's just talk about this later okay?

*

BERNADETTE. Listen, I've got a presentation tomorrow. Can we talk about this later?

*

OLIVER. Just stop, just stop. I think it'd be better if we talked about this... when we've cooled off a bit.

*

BERNADETTE. I've got to go, I'm late. We'll just talk about it later.

*

OLIVER. I think it's really important we talk about this and I'm glad you brought it up.

*

BERNADETTE. I really do want to talk about it though.

*

OLIVER. Yeah.

*

BERNADETTE. Yeah.

*

Voices raised:

BERNADETTE. Yes you were – you were! You were implying, to my fucking boss, that I'm a ticking time bomb baby machine. I'm watching him figuring out maternity cover in front of my eyes, taking me off the big cases. We've never even spoken about kids in any real way. No we haven't. Name one time. You got high once and said you wanted a brood and that's fucking it. Oh it was hurtful to you? You're always hurt. You do this 'Oh that's heartbreaking for me, I'm so sensitive' bullshit. I am concentrating on the road –

OLIVER. I wasn't saying anything like that! No, come on – that's totally distorting! Jesus – watch the road. Ugh you always twist everything I – No, I said it was something that I, me, autonomous-person-me wanted at some point in my life. I've said that loads of times to you! Yes, we have and you didn't say anything and it was really hurtful to me. I wasn't high. I'd had a drink cos I was nervous to talk to you about it. Oh you're just cold, Bernadette. You're a cold person. Concentrate on the –

A sudden intake of breath.

BERNADETTE (*mumbled*). He was… he came out of nowhere.

It's fine. Everyone's fine.

Long pause.

Stop it.

OLIVER. I wasn't saying anything.

BERNADETTE. Sometimes you don't have to say things.

OLIVER. Yeah sometimes.

*

OLIVER. Twelve.

BERNADETTE. Eighteen.

Silence.

OLIVER. This good.

BERNADETTE. Put cayenne in sauce.

OLIVER. Thanks.

Pause.

Hair nice.

BERNADETTE *sighs.*

BERNADETTE. Thanks.

*

OLIVER. We are happy aren't we?

BERNADETTE. Yes.

OLIVER. You're happy?

BERNADETTE. Yes.

OLIVER. And I'm happy.

BERNADETTE. Yes.

OLIVER. Good.

BERNADETTE. When you're happy, you're still not happy all the time are you?

OLIVER. No. That'd be weird.

BERNADETTE. It'd be creepy.

OLIVER. It'd be downright creepy.

BERNADETTE. Yeah. You need light and / shade.

OLIVER. Light and shade. Yeah. Otherwise you'd get sweaty and / overheat.

BERNADETTE. We only argue because we know each other so well.

OLIVER. I'm really glad we're on the same page about this.

BERNADETTE. Me too.

Pause.

BERNADETTE. Why did you and Julie / break up?

OLIVER. Because it was just time.

BERNADETTE. Why was / it time?

OLIVER. There were a whole host of reasons.

Pause.

BERNADETTE. Oliver. I'm sorry that I make more money than you.

*

OLIVER. Well, you know what it is? It's censorship.

BERNADETTE. It's not / censorship.

OLIVER. Of course / it is.

BERNADETTE. It's not censorship. You can say anything you like just… concisely.

OLIVER. That's bullshit, Bernadette.

BERNADETTE. It's not bullshit, Oliver. I'm not saying it's a good law. / It's not. I'm just saying it's not censorship.

OLIVER. You're pussyfooting. Fence-sitting. There are things you can't say in one hundred and forty words.

BERNADETTE. I know that.

OLIVER. Like wedding speeches, or presentations or epic poetry. Songs. A lot of songs have / more than one hundred and forty words in.

BERNADETTE. I'm with you. I agree with you. This was a thing before. Why are you so riled up all of a sudden?

OLIVER. Apparently there's real movement in the Nay camp and a / good few are considering

BERNADETTE. There's no movement in the Nay camp. It's been the same for months. Ever since they got in. Before / even.

OLIVER. Hip hop is as good as dead.

BERNADETTE. They're talking about a daily limit. Hip hop artists can record half a song one day then come in the next day to do the rest.

OLIVER. It'll cost too much. Studio time is fucking expensive. The big names will be fine but the young ones…

BERNADETTE. Well maybe they'll waive it in special circumstances.

OLIVER. What? Like your fancy divorce trials.

BERNADETTE. No.

OLIVER. You know what it does? It alienates the working class.

BERNADETTE. Does it?

OLIVER. It's elitist.

BERNADETTE. How? Everyone gets the same / number of

OLIVER. Yes everyone gets the same number of words but it's the working classes that need them most. The powerful stay powerful because nobody's got enough words to challenge them, nepotism multiplies exponentially and becomes basically the only way of getting jobs because well, who's got enough words for interviews? Social mobility doesn't exist in this. Class mobility is… it's polarised. It's all polarised. Protest is banned. They're cutting the working class off like a bad bit of meat. Like how do they rise up? How do you say 'Hello you, everyone, hello, I'm here and I'm fucking good,' you know. I'm good. Nobody can tell each other they're good any more. But if you've got money you're fine because you *wear* it don't you? You *wear* it in your clothes and in the way you walk, and in the buildings that you go into and come out of. But the working class – Jesus! – the working class can't get through the door. You know *you* should be angry about this Bernadette.

BERNADETTE. Why's that, Oliver? Because I'm one of them?

OLIVER. Everyone should be angry about this.

BERNADETTE. Don't patronise me.

OLIVER. They're banning democracy.

BERNADETTE. They're not banning anything.

OLIVER. They're limiting it.

BERNADETTE. Apparently it's been really good in Norway.

OLIVER. For what?

BERNADETTE. For errr... okay so, since Quietude / came in:

OLIVER. Hate that word. Euphemistic... / think-tank... nothing.

BERNADETTE. Workplace bullying has gone down. Drunk texting is basically over. People are eating more root vegetables for some reason?

OLIVER (*sarcastic*). Sounds like some rock-solid data.

BERNADETTE. Oliver you're being

OLIVER. I'm being rightfully angry. They're using this faux-benevolent bullshit about 'wellbeing' and 'overstimulation' to lock us all up in some... linguistic... gulag.

BERNADETTE. Where are you getting this from?

OLIVER....The news? And, y'know, my thoughts.

Beat.

BERNADETTE. Look, I'm not saying that everyone backing it has like, positive motives but some of them seem to really want what's best for –

OLIVER. So they're either evil or deluded. Great.

BERNADETTE. You're in favour of limits on other things.

OLIVER. This isn't fracking, Bernadette. We're not pumping toxins into the ether. There are no negative externalities to chatting.

BERNADETTE (*quietly, eyebrows raised*). Really?

OLIVER. Plus words aren't a finite resource. We're not running out of them. There's no natural limit to how much / you can say.

BERNADETTE. There's a natural limit to how much you can listen to.

OLIVER.... well that's not entirely... / At any one time, sure, but –

BERNADETTE. There's a natural limit to how much *I* can listen to.

Beat.

OLIVER. I wasn't patronising you.

BERNADETTE. Okay.

OLIVER. I didn't mean to.

BERNADETTE. Okay.

OLIVER. I just think that you, you know, come from a certain background and they, right now, need some sticking up for but, of the two of us, it's me that's really / trying to

BERNADETTE. What, that's gracing us working-class people with his support?

OLIVER. No.

BERNADETTE. You're not a better person than me.

OLIVER. I know that.

BERNADETTE. I'm a lawyer.

Pause.

OLIVER. What do you mean by that?

BERNADETTE.... I dunno.

Beat.

OLIVER. Well there are lots of people who haven't been as lucky as

BERNADETTE. I'm not lucky.

OLIVER. Alright, who haven't worked as hard as you have maybe but I don't think they deserve to be cut out by a law that limits how much they can say.

BERNADETTE. How much everyone can say.

OLIVER. Yes, how much everyone can say. But it takes more words if you don't have money, Bernadette.

BERNADETTE. You're asking me to talk as if I represent like millions of very different people / from very different –

OLIVER. I'm not asking you to talk like anything. We're just chatting. We're just having a conversation.

BERNADETTE. Then why do I feel like I'm on *Newsnight*?

OLIVER. People can talk about serious things without being on *Newsnight*.

BERNADETTE. I am not my background.

OLIVER. I know that.

BERNADETTE. No, I'm not my background.

OLIVER (*robotically*). Yes, and you're not a lawyer and you're not my girlfriend. You're little bits of / all of those things.

BERNADETTE. I'm little bits of all those things and yes, more and I'm not something that is finished. Soon, now, even, I'm going to be little bits of other things as well and you're going to have to be okay with that.

OLIVER. I know that.

BERNADETTE. Do you?

OLIVER. Yeah I didn't mean…

BERNADETTE. It's a bad law. I don't think it's going to pass.

OLIVER. How are you going to explain all of those little things in one hundred and forty words?

BERNADETTE. Maybe I'm not going to explain it.

OLIVER. Then nobody's gonna know who you are.

BERNADETTE. Well... I don't...

OLIVER. People are just going to make limiting, confining assumptions / about –

BERNADETTE. I was agreeing with you, Oliver. It's a bad law. It's a bad law. I don't think it's going to pass.

OLIVER. Good.

BERNADETTE. Hey.

OLIVER. I'm going on the march tomorrow.

BERNADETTE. I thought we were gonna go swimming.

*

BERNADETTE. Twenty-six.

OLIVER. 123,205,750.

Beat.

BERNADETTE. You've improved.

OLIVER. Words humans use in lifetime.

BERNADETTE. A lot.

OLIVER. Used to.

BERNADETTE. Now?

OLIVER. 4,011,350

BERNADETTE. Still a lot.

OLIVER. If talking from birth.

BERNADETTE. Unlikely.

OLIVER. 119,195,400 gone.

BERNADETTE. Memorised?

OLIVER. Per person. Per lifetime. Extinct.

BERNADETTE. Melodramatic.

OLIVER. Sad. Really sad.

Pause.

BERNADETTE. Qualifiers. They can go first.

*

OLIVER. I'm busy on Friday.

Pause.

BERNADETTE. You're busy Friday.

OLIVER. I'm busy Friday.

BERNADETTE. Why are you busy Friday?

OLIVER. Okay right well, listen. They want us quiet. Hushed. That's the point, that's the point of the law, right? So I thought noise. Noise.

BERNADETTE. …noise?

OLIVER. Noise. Doesn't matter what we're saying. Doesn't matter how. We don't even need to be saying anything. Word-wise. Just need to be loud. And it's actually happening on Friday. It was just this thing that I thought of and now it's… Thousands of people screaming through London. We're bringing horns, gongs, trumpets. A couple of guys are bringing a timpani set on a wheelie-platform. They're gonna take turns pushing the platform and playing the drums.

BERNADETTE. But aren't you proving them right?

OLIVER. Who?

BERNADETTE. Them. Capital T-H them.

OLIVER. How?

BERNADETTE. Walking through London shouting your heads off.

OLIVER. Of course not, we're being free and using, you know, the human rights that we have.

BERNADETTE. Oh right. Yes. Of course.

OLIVER. You'll be able to hear us from space. Space.

BERNADETTE. But there's nobody in space.

OLIVER. Bernadette. You will be able to hear our protest march from space. I mean that is... sick. That's a fucking cool protest march if you can hear it from... Democracy is all about...

BERNADETTE. What is democracy all about, Oliver?

Pause.

OLIVER. Democracy is about voices being heard. On Friday our voices are going to be heard through Westminster, across the Channel, across the whole freaking world and, yes, into space. And, Bernadette, it was kind of all my idea.

BERNADETTE. Isn't there no sound in space?

Pause.

OLIVER. I don't think that's right.

*

BERNADETTE. Forty-three.

OLIVER. Forty-three.

They note the unlikeliness.

Silence.

They look at each other. Something is happening.

BERNADETTE. Is it now?

Pause.

OLIVER. 'is it now'

He shakes his head as if saying 'I have no idea' to himself.

Beat.

BERNADETTE. Don't want. But

OLIVER. Talk.

BERNADETTE. Conversation.

OLIVER. Yeah.

*

BERNADETTE. Coverage was great.

OLIVER. Yeah.

BERNADETTE. Really. The coverage was everywhere.

OLIVER. Not too bad, yeah.

BERNADETTE. You looked handsome on TV.

OLIVER. Thanks. Jealous?

BERNADETTE. What? No. Of course not. I'm sorry about how we left it this morning.

OLIVER. Oh, don't be.

Pause.

BERNADETTE. Are you happy with it?

OLIVER. With what?

BERNADETTE. The protest.

OLIVER. Well it's not really about me being happy with it.

BERNADETTE. Isn't it?

Pause.

OLIVER. Bernadette.

BERNADETTE. Mmmm.

OLIVER. I need to... I'm really...

BERNADETTE. What?

OLIVER. I don't really know how to say...

BERNADETTE. Oliver.

OLIVER. I'm really sorry.

BERNADETTE. Reeeeeaaaally?

OLIVER (*steely*). Bernadette.

Silence.

BERNADETTE. What?

OLIVER. Today erm…

Pause.

BERNADETTE. What?

OLIVER. Please don't hate me. I think that would be probably more than I could, you know… take I guess.

BERNADETTE. What did you do?

OLIVER. I mean I know you do sometimes. Hate me. But it's always… fleeting. It's always short bursts of hate and even when I think it's going to be longer than that it isn't. But even those sometimes feel like deserts.

BERNADETTE. Oliver. What did you do?

Pause.

OLIVER. Julie was at the march. She… I tried to… I didn't try that hard.

Silence.

BERNADETTE *nods and turns away.*

We threw a brick through a window.

BERNADETTE. What?

OLIVER. Yeah. We threw a brick through a window.

BERNADETTE. You threw a brick through a window?

OLIVER. Yep. Of a WHSmith.

BERNADETTE. You threw a brick through the window of a WHSmith.

OLIVER. We did. I mean we threw a brick each. We didn't throw one together. I don't even know how you'd go about that. Probably wouldn't be a very good throw if we'd done that. In terms of power or accuracy.

BERNADETTE. That was the thing.

OLIVER. What? Yep. That was the thing.

BERNADETTE. Oh.

OLIVER. Yep. We didn't get caught or anything but I knew you'd be annoyed.

BERNADETTE. Yeah, I am... Oliver. I'm really...

Silence.

(*Firmly.*) I love you.

OLIVER. I love you too.

Pause.

Bernadette –

BERNADETTE. I'm glad it was only one brick. Not like several bricks.

Beat.

OLIVER. Yeah.

Pause.

*

OLIVER. Forty-six.

BERNADETTE. Ten.

OLIVER. Okay. Right. I need to just tell you this now... it's been killing me and –

BERNADETTE. No, don't.

OLIVER. Bernadette, at the noise march, I –

BERNADETTE. Stop.

OLIVER. I need to –

BERNADETTE. Oliver, don't. Got nothing to give back.

*

BERNADETTE. Morning.

OLIVER. Morning.

BERNADETTE. How are you feeling?

OLIVER. Okay.

BERNADETTE. Good.

OLIVER. We've done all we could.

BERNADETTE. You have.

OLIVER. If they're gonna pass this fascist fest of a law now, they were always going to.

Pause.

You don't think it's fascist.

BERNADETTE. I don't.

OLIVER. How can you think that?

BERNADETTE. I'm different from you.

Pause.

OLIVER. You're gonna be late to work.

BERNADETTE. They've cancelled it.

OLIVER. They've cancelled it?

BERNADETTE. All the courts are shut today. For the vote.

Beat.

OLIVER. That makes sense. This is more important, I suppose.

Silence.

*

OLIVER. Turn it on.

BERNADETTE. Okay.

OLIVER. Here we go.

BERNADETTE. Here we go.

Long silence. It should feel potentially endless.

OLIVER. Turn it off.

Silence.

BERNADETTE. I'm gonna have to gag myself at night.

OLIVER. What?

BERNADETTE. I talk in my sleep. How many times have you told me I talk in my sleep. I'm gonna have to gag myself at night with like duct tape or a sock or something. Otherwise I'm just wasting. Just being wasteful.

OLIVER. Yeah.

BERNADETTE. I never thought they'd actually…

OLIVER. Yeah.

BERNADETTE. Go through with it.

OLIVER. Yeah.

BERNADETTE. And how can they… how can it go through so

OLIVER. Soon. Yeah.

BERNADETTE. Monday.

OLIVER. They knew it was gonna pass.

BERNADETTE. They can't have. It was too close.

OLIVER. They had the votes.

BERNADETTE. I'm sorry, Oliver.

OLIVER. What for?

BERNADETTE. *How* did I not…

'Unforgivable.'

Pause.

Okay. Right. So we've got errrm we've got four days, four and a bit days before you know, it kicks in. I really think it's important that we make the most of it. We should make the most of it. Because one hundred and forty words a day isn't a lot of words and I know I'll have to use most of them at work and you'll have to, yes, use some of yours as well. So it'll be hard for us to talk and communicate. You know, like we do.

Pause.

But I guess it's lucky we've already got each other.

OLIVER. Yeah, and that we already know each other so well.

BERNADETTE. Cos meeting someone new would be...

OLIVER. Like thank *God*, you know.

BERNADETTE. Yeah.

OLIVER. I need to make a speech.

BERNADETTE. Oh / right, okay.

OLIVER. To the, to the losers, I guess. Thanking them and... I guess encouraging them to keep going / because maybe there's a

BERNADETTE. I don't know if this is something that you can just get repealed.

OLIVER. But if there was like, overwhelming public outrage, they'd have to. Right?

BERNADETTE. Yeah. Uh. It's hard from a legal perspective but...

OLIVER. But they wouldn't have a choice would they?

BERNADETTE (*unconvincingly*)....Maybe!

OLIVER. Okay, honestly: do you think there's any real chance of overturning this?

Pause. She looks at him.

BERNADETTE. Yeah... Yeah! A chance.

OLIVER. Yeah?

BERNADETTE. If there was overwhelming

OLIVER. In like six months or something?

BERNADETTE. Yeah. Six months. Sure.

OLIVER. Okay. Okay I'm gonna

BERNADETTE. Yeah. Go.

Beat.

They look at each other, panting, full of adrenalin.

If something funny happens on the way to the supermarket I might not be able to tell you about it.

OLIVER. I know.

BERNADETTE. Or at least it would... it would come at a price.

OLIVER. Yeah.

BERNADETTE. I didn't... I hadn't thought about that.

Beat.

Then they come together and kiss.

There's a kind of feverish warmth about it.

OLIVER. I'm gonna go and then I'll come right back here and we'll spend the next four days figuring this out.

BERNADETTE. Okay.

OLIVER. We need to find ways around it. Tricks and things.

Beat.

BERNADETTE. Tricks and things.

*

BERNADETTE. What about abbreviations?

OLIVER. Abbreviations?

BERNADETTE. Like can't or don't or wasn't or weren't or...

OLIVER. What about them?

BERNADETTE. Do they count as one or two?

OLIVER. Oh right. Well how many do they count as on phones and computers.

BERNADETTE. We should check.

OLIVER. They count as one!

BERNADETTE. Come on!

OLIVER. So you can say can't and still have one hundred and thirty-nine left.

BERNADETTE. Well that's a relief.

OLIVER. I feel relieved.

BERNADETTE. Like a weight's been lifted.

OLIVER. A little bit like a weight's been lifted, yes.

BERNADETTE. Like a light weight.

OLIVER. Maybe we should like... Maybe we should just create a whole load of new abbreviations? That halves our output.

BERNADETTE. Like a code?

OLIVER. Yes. Sort of. So, so instead of 'sort of' we could just say 'sorf'.

BERNADETTE. 'Sorf.'

OLIVER. Yeah.

BERNADETTE. Or instead of 'instead of' we could say 'insteaf'.

OLIVER. Exactly.

BERNADETTE. Or instead of 'see you later' we could have er... we could say... 'seeouayer'.

OLIVER. Well, I mean that's one's a bit... You could just say 'seeya'.

BERNADETTE. Yeah. I like that. That's better.

OLIVER. And instead of saying 'how are you' or 'how was your day' we could just say: 'how?'

BERNADETTE. But what if we're asking a different how-related question. Like how does this microwave oven work? Or how do I stop my mum and brother from murdering each other?

OLIVER. Okay.

BERNADETTE. Or how do you pronounce a double-L in Welsh?

OLIVER. Okay that one wasn't… But I guess they'll emerge.

BERNADETTE. Yeah.

OLIVER. In our daily lives.

BERNADETTE. In our day-to-day.

OLIVER. Yes. Good.

BERNADETTE. Instead of 'I love you' we could say 'lovou'.

OLIVER. Yes. Definitely. Exactly.

*

OLIVER. Morse code! We could speak in Morse code!

BERNADETTE. How does that work?

OLIVER. Okay so each letter is a combination of dots and dashes.

BERNADETTE. Right.

OLIVER. So like an S is three dots.

BERNADETTE. Dot dot dot. That's three words for one letter.

OLIVER. No, no, we'd tap it.

OLIVER *dives onto the floor and taps three times*.

BERNADETTE. Oliver.

OLIVER. Shhhhh.

Come on, we can't write things down either so if we're out and we need to... y'know... what are we gonna do?

BERNADETTE. Okay.

He taps the floor three times.

S.

OLIVER *smiles widely.*

How do you do a dash?

OLIVER *drags his finger across the floor.*

OLIVER. I'll get you a book on it.

BERNADETTE. Thanks.

*

OLIVER *reads from a list.*

OLIVER. Alright things to move until after the repeal:

BERNADETTE (*uncertainly*). Yeah.

OLIVER. Likely repeal.

BERNADETTE. Yep.

OLIVER. Hopeful repeal.

BERNADETTE. Mmhmm.

OLIVER. Recording the vocals on my new –

BERNADETTE. Yep. Sadly. Cos I was excited to hear –

OLIVER. The whole Starting Therapy idea.

BERNADETTE. Definitely. Errrrr... learning French for me.

OLIVER. Bien sûr.

BERNADETTE. Nice.

OLIVER. De rien.

BERNADETTE. Show-off.

OLIVER. I've got all 'Shall We Get Married' chat.

BERNADETTE. Yep yep yep. Very boring wedding.

OLIVER. Sparse.

BERNADETTE. Don't get to hear how much everyone loves us.

Beat. OLIVER *gives her a look.*

...or how much we love each other.

OLIVER. 'Arguments'? What do we reckon?

BERNADETTE (*laughing*). Yep, won't be needing those. Oooh babies! No babies while the limit's in.

OLIVER. Oh. Um. Okay. Yep.

BERNADETTE. Not that we're necessarily close to that / anyway

OLIVER. No, / but

BERNADETTE. But you'd wanna be able to talk to the...

OLIVER. Presumably babies will take a lot longer to learn to talk.

BERNADETTE. Yeah, or they'll just be very concise from a very young age.

OLIVER. Playgrounds full of concise babies looking at each other intently... and then saying, like... 'Dinosaurs'.

BERNADETTE. Either way...

OLIVER. Yeah.

BERNADETTE. Kick that one down the curb. Blast it off into space.

OLIVER. There's obviously a slight time limit on...

BERNADETTE. Wow. Alright.

OLIVER. Not that you're

BERNADETTE. Not that I'm...?

OLIVER. It just gets harder doesn't it?

BERNADETTE. Does it?

OLIVER. Like medically...

BERNADETTE. It's gonna be six months!

OLIVER. Hopefully.

BERNADETTE. It's fine. I'm... very... I'm full of 'em.

OLIVER. Cool.

BERNADETTE. Get us out the hole, Oliver.

OLIVER. Sorry.

Pause. They smile at each other.

'Mumbling.'

*

OLIVER. Maybe we'll just have to look into each other's eyes more. Eye contact. You can do a lot with eye contact.

BERNADETTE. Yeah.

OLIVER. Like people tell whole stories with their eyes.

BERNADETTE. Do they?

OLIVER. I mean metaphorically.

BERNADETTE. Right. Yep.

OLIVER. Like, now, let's try, look in my eyes – what am I...

BERNADETTE. What are you thinking?

OLIVER. Yeah.

He's staring at her incredibly intensely.

BERNADETTE. Working out where to hide the body?

Beat.

Working out where to hide *my* body?

OLIVER. Come on.

BERNADETTE. Okay you're thinking I look pretty fucking *smoking* in these trackie bottoms.

OLIVER. Bang on.

*

BERNADETTE. I was thinking

OLIVER. Mmm?

BERNADETTE. About the repeal

OLIVER. Yeah.

BERNADETTE. It's gonna be

OLIVER. Hard.

BERNADETTE. Not impossible! But

OLIVER. Difficult.

BERNADETTE. Yeah.

OLIVER. Legally speaking.

BERNADETTE. But what I think you could do – what I think is more likely to work in the short term at least, is trying to attach some kind of amendment.

OLIVER. Okay.

BERNADETTE. About events or spaces where the limit is um… is, like, suspended.

OLIVER. Oh. Okay. They'd never go for recording studios though.

BERNADETTE. No but

OLIVER. But protests!

BERNADETTE. Exactly.

OLIVER. Well…well, that's a great idea!

BERNADETTE. Yeah?

OLIVER. Yeah that's brilliant.

Beat.

BERNADETTE. Thanks.

*

Slowly. A little dazed.

BERNADETTE. Maybe we'll read more.

OLIVER. That'd be good.

BERNADETTE. Yeah.

Pause.

OLIVER. I mean, surely we'll read more.

BERNADETTE. Yeah. Cos what else –

OLIVER. Exactly.

Pause.

BERNADETTE. Well that's a little bit of a silver lining right there.

OLIVER. Mmm. Always mean to read more.

*

BERNADETTE. How long have we got?

OLIVER. About five minutes.

BERNADETTE. And then...

OLIVER. Yeah.

BERNADETTE. Okay. I want to... I want to say everything then...

OLIVER. Yeah.

BERNADETTE. I want to just say everything, okay?

OLIVER. Yeah.

BERNADETTE. Everything that I've ever wanted to say but never been really able to for some reason or other. And

everything that you Oliver that you've always wanted to say
but never really been able to say for some reason or other.

OLIVER. Yes.

BERNADETTE. I don't want to talk later.

OLIVER. Well it'll be difficult to talk later.

BERNADETTE. We'd have to do it in Morse code.

OLIVER. Yes, it would be slow.

BERNADETTE. Okay I'll start.

OLIVER. Right. Okay.

BERNADETTE. I'm gonna start.

OLIVER. Whenever you're ready.

BERNADETTE. You start.

OLIVER. Okay.

BERNADETTE. We'll take it in turns or yeah just see how it
goes.

OLIVER. Right. Errrm. Okay. I love you. I do. I'm very
grateful for you being with me and indulging me I guess in
all my little things that I errrm... And I know I like to play
the victim sometimes and I like to sulk and I like to punish
you if you've done things wrong. Well I don't *like* to punish
you I just do sometimes – I'm not very forgiving. I know that
and I'm sorry for that, I am, I am sorry for that because it,
you know, probably has some repercussions on you and your
state of mind and on us and...

BERNADETTE. Cool. Cool. Yep. Keep going.

OLIVER. And sometimes I feel that you don't listen to what I'm
saying or no you do listen, you do but you always have other
cogs whirring at the same time if you know what I mean? Like
if you were a laptop you'd have other tabs open. If you were
an internet browser I mean. Like you're looking at me, you're
definitely looking at me and focusing on me but but but you're

aware that at the top of the page there are, you know, other things open, other tabs. Maybe you've got Facebook or the news or a couple of YouTube videos about cats...

BERNADETTE. Yep doesn't matter, keep going.

OLIVER. And I don't like your brother. I think he is too dismissive of you and, yes, of me as well, and he's too actually, you know what, and you're going to disagree with me here, but too self-involved. I think he is so paranoid about retaining absolute control of every little thing he does that he's actually a bit rude and also, also, very hard to buy presents for on birthdays.

BERNADETTE. Yep, agree about the birthday thing, not the rest.

OLIVER. Yes, well, I thought that was the point. You said you wanted us to just say...

BERNADETTE. No no it was. That's good, that's so good, that's so good. I'll go now.

OLIVER. Great.

BERNADETTE. Okay. Cool. Yep. Right. Sometimes I feel like, and I know I've said this a million times, but that you think I'm shallow.

OLIVER. Right. Yep. Good.

BERNADETTE. No, I do, I do. And also bad. You make me feel like I'm bad. You're always higher than me. For some reason, you're always higher. It's like when we started we decided that you were going to be the good person and I was going to be the bad person. Even though sometimes, occasionally I feel pretty strongly that I'm actually the good person and you, you're the er... And not just in the heat of the moment, I look back on it and I think about it and I reflect and reason with myself and I still think that *there*, just there, not always, but just there I was the good... one.

OLIVER. Wonderful.

BERNADETTE. Oliver.

OLIVER. No, no carry on. It's good that we're airing these while we've got this errr... fleeting window of opportunity.

BERNADETTE. See there! Just there! This fleeting window of opportunity. What is that? The way you say things. Sometimes I think you use big words to make yourself feel better and me feel worse. Is it some kind of male-dominance thing because my paycheque is bigger than yours? Is it you saying 'I'm doing what I love because I love it, you, you're a sell-out, you're driven by money and security, but me, well, if I wanted to sell out and be a fucking lawyer then I'd use all these like, abstract concepts in court and people would listen to what I was saying because I'm clever in an obvious way.' A lot of what you say sounds like that sometimes. A lot of our conversations feel like that.

OLIVER. Cool. Coool. Errr can I jump back in here or have you got more to...

BERNADETTE. Yeah do it! Go for it!

OLIVER. This is good stuff. Real exorcising stuff.

BERNADETTE. Mmmhmm. Quickly.

OLIVER. So I don't like what you do. I know you think I don't like it and I know you hate me for that and for not understanding that your mum worked in Tesco and your dad barely worked so you have this thing about achievement. And I love you for that. Sure. And I know you *think* you always wanted to be a lawyer but come on, like you must have had passions and stuff and...

BERNADETTE. Okay. Great. I really feel like we're making... like we're getting all this stuff out. It's like an exorcism. We just get through and then puff it's gone.

OLIVER. Yeah, definitely. Puff.

BERNADETTE. Is there anything else?

OLIVER. Nope.

BERNADETTE. Really?

Pause.

OLIVER. Nope.

BERNADETTE. Because if there is anything… It's about to be really hard for us to –

OLIVER. That's all.

BERNADETTE. Right. Okay. Great.

OLIVER. Oh and I love you.

BERNADETTE. Yep, I've got something else.

OLIVER. Well we've barely got any time left so…

BERNADETTE. So in bed. Sometimes, sometimes in bed. Okay I know that you… you do this whole *love* thing. And you're staring in my eyes. Like right in my eyes… While you're… you know. And it's a bit… and I like that you're so responsive to me and caring and intent on me, you know… And it is *so* nice. Boy is it nice! Really. But sometimes I'm just a bit… I dunno… it's hard to think of the right word. Now, bored isn't the right word.

OLIVER. Okay yep faster. Much faster now. Come on. Thirty seconds. Faster faster faster.

BERNADETTE. And I wish you'd just stop fiddling around and worrying about… and just… let loose and really give it something, cowboy. Sometimes I want to feel sexy and powerful and like we could be in *Basic Instinct* or *Brokeback Mountain* or… I wish you'd just have at me once or twice. I don't want to be sensitive or lovey, I don't want to feel like your entire life had been leading up to the moment that you put your thing in my… I want you to be strong and…

OLIVER. And wrap it up, wrap it up.

BERNADETTE. But I like that we are, you know, making progress as a couple because what's a relationship if it's not moving… you know and I'm excited, I'm really excited about…

OLIVER. Stop stop stop stop stop!

A very long silence.

They both breathe out slowly.

BERNADETTE. Lovou.

OLIVER. Lovou.

Pause.

Bed?

BERNADETTE *smiles.*

BERNADETTE. You.

She nods emphatically and points.

I.

She breathes out and pushes the palms of her hands downwards as if to say 'I need a moment.'

OLIVER *smiles and nods.*

*

OLIVER. I'm sorry but are you okay?

BERNADETTE (*teary*). Yeah, no I'm fine. / I'm just very

OLIVER. I'm really sorry for your loss.

BERNADETTE. What?

OLIVER. Dennis. I'm really sorry that you had to go through that. I was at the protest. Where he was you know… crushed. It all got a bit out of hand, if I'm honest. Oh no, but I wasn't / involved

BERNADETTE. No Dennis wasn't my…

OLIVER (*talking over her*). I tried to save Dennis but couldn't get through the crowd fast enough. I am so sorry. Honestly. I was only there for a friend really. She's super against the Hush Law, / you see so…

BERNADETTE. No. Dennis wasn't my cat. He was Steph's.

OLIVER. You're not Steph.

BERNADETTE. No.

OLIVER. I just thought... because you were crying...

BERNADETTE. I was very moved.

OLIVER. Oh. Right.

BERNADETTE. I thought it was a beautiful service and I was very moved. I used to be a cold bitch but I had a friend die a couple of years ago and now I can't lose like, a *jacket* without setting off the sprinklers.

OLIVER. Oh. That's really hard.

I lost a jacket when I was twelve and I carry that with me every day.

BERNADETTE *laughs*.

BERNADETTE. Seriously, last week I was in the supermarket and I saw an old man plucking a single banana off a bunch – floods.

OLIVER. I'm sorry about your friend.

BERNADETTE. Oh did you kill him?

OLIVER *laughs*. *She smiles*.

Beat.

OLIVER. So you know Steph?

BERNADETTE. Yeah. You?

OLIVER. Well I thought you were her so...

BERNADETTE. Why are you here then?

OLIVER. Well, I felt bad about the... guilty I guess for being... Oh and I know Dan who did the errr... I guess you'd call it a eulogy.

BERNADETTE. Oh. Tell him I thought it was beautiful.

OLIVER. Dan's very good at finding things to say about cats.

BERNADETTE. That's quite a skill.

OLIVER. I didn't even know they had pet cemeteries. Eerily quiet isn't it.

Beat.

He worked on one of my tracks actually. Dan.

BERNADETTE (*a joke*). Oh you work on the railroads.

Beat. OLIVER *looks confused.*

You're a musician you're a musician.

OLIVER. Yeah. Well recently it's just been jingles for adverts mainly but...

BERNADETTE. Anything I'd know?

OLIVER. Probably not.

BERNADETTE. I'm a lawyer.

OLIVER. Oh. Right. Okay. Yeah / that's... that's really impressive, I guess.

BERNADETTE. Yeah. Well I'm doing my pupillage. Training.

OLIVER. You kind of one-upped me there.

BERNADETTE. Yours is much cooler.

OLIVER. Thanks.

BERNADETTE. What's the Hush Law?

OLIVER. What?

BERNADETTE. You were on a march?

OLIVER. It was for the limit thing. The daily-word-/limit

BERNADETTE. Oh the Quietude Bill. Right yeah I didn't know / it was called that

OLIVER. Yeah. Yeah it's a nickname. My friend basically runs the campaign. So I go with her.

BERNADETTE. She sounds impressive.

OLIVER. She's okay.

Pause.

What's your name?

BERNADETTE. Bernadette.

OLIVER. Wow.

BERNADETTE. What?

OLIVER. No. It's just that that's not a name you hear... Like I've never... Y'know I don't think I've *ever* met a Bernadette before. You're now my original Bernadette. The root from which all others descend.

BERNADETTE. That sounds like a lot of pressure.

What's your name?

OLIVER. Oliver.

BERNADETTE. Ah. I've met tons of them.

Pause.

You don't know me.

OLIVER. Well, I'd like to try.

*

OLIVER *waves at* BERNADETTE.

She waves back.

They speak excessively slowly and loudly (Brits-abroad style). Choosing each word carefully.

BERNADETTE. How was your day?

OLIVER. Weird.

BERNADETTE. Weird how?

OLIVER. Eerie.

BERNADETTE. Yeah.

OLIVER. Quiet.

BERNADETTE. Kind of nice.

OLIVER. It's horrible. Orwellian.

BERNADETTE. Like pet cemetery everywhere.

OLIVER. Your day?

BERNADETTE. How was my…?

OLIVER. Yes.

BERNADETTE. Fine. Spent forty words ordering smoothie.

OLIVER laughs.

Your…?

OLIVER. Met with team. Strategising.

BERNADETTE. Great! What's next?

OLIVER. Pitched your Protest Amendment. Extra words for… during…

BERNADETTE. And?

OLIVER. They loved it! Gonna concentrate efforts on it.

BERNADETTE. That's great.

He nods enthusiastically. BERNADETTE *turns away. Busies herself.*

Partners backing case for extra in courthouses.

OLIVER. Oh.

Pause.

So, everybody's…

BERNADETTE. Tooting their own...

OLIVER. Yeah.

Pause. OLIVER *seems to be growing prickly.*

All courthouses?

BERNADETTE *shrugs.*

Understand for bad... y'know... but for like: non-criminal, *vanity*

BERNADETTE. Words.

Beat.

OLIVER. We'll see.

BERNADETTE. Yeah.

OLIVER. What until then?

BERNADETTE. Nobody knows.

Beat.

OLIVER. Nobody knows.

*

Playing Articulate again.

BERNADETTE. Cairo!

OLIVER *shakes his head.*

Alexandria!

OLIVER *nods and gives her the thumbs-up.*

He takes another deep breath in.

OLIVER. Pushing down. Emotionally.

BERNADETTE. Forgetting.

He shakes his head.

Repressing.

He gestures as if to say 'close'.

Lying.

OLIVER *shakes his head.*

Lying.

OLIVER *shakes his head again.*

I don't know.

OLIVER. Suppressing. Come on.

BERNADETTE. Lying same thing.

OLIVER. Good training

She nods.

We're getting better.

BERNADETTE. Need be more honest with each other.

*

OLIVER *and* BERNADETTE *stare purposefully into each other's eyes.*

They move their eyes theatrically as if trying to tell a story.

This goes on for a long time.

*

Silence.

BERNADETTE. When I wake up, just for a second I…

OLIVER. Forget.

BERNADETTE. Yeah.

Silence.

*

OLIVER. This one says: Bella, you were the light of my life and you loved tuna.

BERNADETTE. Jasper, a really good cat. Often mistaken for meatloaf.

OLIVER. Maybe that was how he died. Maybe he was accidentally baked.

BERNADETTE. Dennis, a cat full of joy. If he could talk, he'd sing.

OLIVER. Dan's good / at talking about cats.

BERNADETTE. Dan's good at talking about cats.

OLIVER. What would you put?

BERNADETTE. Something very clever and witty.

OLIVER. Seriously.

BERNADETTE. Seriously I'd just put how much I loved them. What else is there.

Pause.

What?

Pause.

OLIVER. You're refreshing. I find you refreshing.

BERNADETTE. I'm not refreshing.

OLIVER. You're a lawyer.

BERNADETTE. I'm a family / lawyer. In training.

OLIVER. You're a divorce lawyer.

BERNADETTE. They mean the same thing.

OLIVER. We both know which one sounds nicer.

BERNADETTE. Maybe if it sounds nicer it is nicer.

OLIVER (*teasing*). Or maybe it's just a friendly name for a painful thing.

Beat.

BERNADETTE. We should go.

OLIVER. Where do you / wanna go?

BERNADETTE. I should go.

OLIVER. I'm sorry if I've…

Pause.

You're giving me that look.

BERNADETTE. What look?

OLIVER. I just went through a break-up so I'm pretty familiar with that look.

BERNADETTE. You didn't mention that.

OLIVER. When would I have mentioned it? I don't know your last name yet.

BERNADETTE. Oh I don't have one.

OLIVER *laughs*.

What look?

OLIVER. You know, when you're standing across from each other after some dumb argument or whatever and it's like: is it now?

BERNADETTE. 'Is it now?'

OLIVER. Yeah.

BERNADETTE. 'Is what now?'

OLIVER. The beginning of the end.

Beat.

BERNADETTE. I'm not your life raft.

OLIVER. I know.

BERNADETTE. We just met.

OLIVER. I know.

I'm really sorry for saying…

BERNADETTE. Usually I love calling myself a lawyer. Wearing that as a kind of… I dunno. And seeing how people's expressions change. Their body language. But then sometimes I start to hate it. I don't really know why.

OLIVER. It can be both.

Beat.

Thanks for telling me that though.

Beat.

Same look or different look?

BERNADETTE. You have nice eyes.

*

BERNADETTE. Tired?

OLIVER. Yeah.

BERNADETTE. Not in the mood to...?

OLIVER. What?

BERNADETTE. It's been a while.

OLIVER. No. I'm... I could be.

BERNADETTE. Okay.

They breathe deeply.

Ow.

OLIVER. Sorry.

BERNADETTE. No.

OLIVER. What you want me to do?

BERNADETTE. Just...

Pause.

Yeah. Gently. Ow.

OLIVER. I'm sorry. Just tell me...

BERNADETTE. I'm running low.

OLIVER. Same

They breathe deeply again.

BERNADETTE. Ow.

OLIVER. Let's stop.

*

OLIVER. Morning.

BERNADETTE. Morning.

OLIVER. You were talking last night. Through the duct tape. The pens again?

BERNADETTE. Not this time.

Pause.

OLIVER. Meeting new lobbyist today. Lena.

BERNADETTE. Exciting.

OLIVER. Great connections. Promising.

Beat.

BERNADETTE. That's great. Sugar?

OLIVER (*insistent*). Promising.

Beat.

BERNADETTE. Absolutely!

*

OLIVER. Petition's reached

BERNADETTE. Wow!

*

OLIVER. Funding injection

BERNADETTE. Considerable!

*

OLIVER. Opinion polls

BERNADETTE. Glimmers of

                              *

OLIVER. Turnout was

BERNADETTE. Still encouraging!

                              *

OLIVER. The legalities behind

BERNADETTE. Not airtight.

                              *

OLIVER. Lena and Julie at each other's

BERNADETTE. Disagreements productive.

                              *

OLIVER. 'Six months.'

BERNADETTE. Good to be optimistic.

                              *

OLIVER. But you think there's…?

BERNADETTE.…Yeah.

OLIVER. You still think there's…?

BERNADETTE. Yeah.

OLIVER. You do?

    Beat.

BERNADETTE. Yeah.

    Seen about Eliot?

OLIVER. No. Haven't spoken in…

BERNADETTE. Baby born. A girl.

OLIVER (*disbelievingly*). Eliot's a father.

BERNADETTE. It's his second.

OLIVER *reels*.

*

OLIVER. We need to stop meeting here. It's all a bit morbid.

BERNADETTE. Well, it's the only place that I know that you know.

OLIVER. You've never asked where else I know.

BERNADETTE. Well, maybe I just like revisiting the graves of dead cats. Maybe I'm just that kind of girl.

OLIVER. Maybe we should talk about other places we could meet.

Pause.

I told my friend Eliot about you.

*

BERNADETTE. Home.

OLIVER. Day?

BERNADETTE *says nothing, in her own world.*

Day?

BERNADETTE. Worst in...

Lost her every...

She trails off. Shakes her head.

OLIVER. Happens.

BERNADETTE. Helpless.

OLIVER. Lena and Julie think amendment / ruling close

BERNADETTE. Think should announce counts when see each other.

OLIVER. Bernadette I was

Beat.

Waste.

BERNADETTE. Gives us an idea of where the other's at.

OLIVER. How many they've saved.

BERNADETTE. How many they've got.

Pause.

OLIVER. Say how many left after...

BERNADETTE. After count. Yeah.

*

OLIVER. Sixteen.

BERNADETTE. Twenty-seven.

*

OLIVER. Fifty-eight.

BERNADETTE. Twenty-three.

*

BERNADETTE. Twenty-nine.

OLIVER. Ninety-two.

*

BERNADETTE. Twenty-two.

OLIVER. One.

*

The early hours of the morning.

OLIVER. Hundred thirty

BERNADETTE. Hundred thirty-eight.

Beat.

Tried t'call.

OLIVER. Turned phone off. After announcement.

Beat.

BERNADETTE. Been worried.

Waiting up. Saving my…

Then, just pre-midnight, used up last twenty reading out back of cereal packet.

He throws her a laugh. It's not as much as she'd hoped.

Pause.

OLIVER. You're very regular. Always in twenties.

BERNADETTE. Try save us some.

OLIVER. Not s'much as can. Just quota.

BERNADETTE. Useful.

OLIVER. Don't want life run by quotas.

BERNADETTE.…okay.

Beat.

OLIVER. Good about courtrooms! Made the list.

BERNADETTE. Yeah.

OLIVER. Partners popping bottles?

BERNADETTE. Pleased.

OLIVER. Lawyers' counts suspended inside courtrooms. Whatever case. Can just…

He makes an open-handed gesture. Like he's releasing something into the sky.

Freely.

Beat.

'Word sanctuaries.'

Weird name.

'Sanctuary.'

Beat.

BERNADETTE. Just practicality issue. Courtroom has walls, set hours. Clear.

Protest – harder to define... parameters.

OLIVER. Yeah.

Pause.

No, I'm happy. You'll save more now.

BERNADETTE *nods. Doesn't look at him. He stares at her for a moment then walks away, busies himself.*

Silence.

BERNADETTE. Can't promise that, Oliver.

Try. But...

He turns to look at her.

Extra *in* courtrooms. Have prep, meetings.

Pause.

OLIVER. Twenty words a day. That's... seven thousand a year?

We spend thirty years together, maybe our conversations fill a couple of newspapers.

Pause.

I miss you.

BERNADETTE. Right here.

OLIVER. Quota of you.

BERNADETTE. All of me.

OLIVER. No.

Can't... access it.

Might as well be... gone.

Beat.

BERNADETTE. Dunderstand.

OLIVER. What?

BERNADETTE. Always punishing…

I didn't… not *my* law.

OLIVER. Did I say it was?

Pause.

BERNADETTE. Can you just… turn it off for a second?

OLIVER. Turn what –

BERNADETTE. *Anger.* It's… all you are.

OLIVER. Necessary. To have chance.

Pause.

She looks at him.

Then sums up the courage.

BERNADETTE (*hard truth*). It's not going away.

OLIVER. What's?

The limit?

BERNADETTE *hesitates then nods.*

So I should give up?

BERNADETTE *looks at the ground.*

What, zero?

BERNADETTE *hesitates then nods. She's lying. Turns away.*

But you had…

(*Realising that she's lying.*) Ah.

Beat.

Well, what a waste.

*

BERNADETTE. Seventy-six. Coffee?

OLIVER. Thirty-two.

   (*Explaining*.) ...phonecall.

   Pause.

BERNADETTE. Sorry for

OLIVER. What's that?

BERNADETTE. Things we moved to after appeal.

   Pause.

OLIVER (*shaking his head*). 'Six months'

BERNADETTE. Kinda sweet?

   OLIVER *grunts, moves away.*

   Yes to coffee?

OLIVER. I stopped drinking it.

BERNADETTE. When?

OLIVER. Ages.

   Pause.

   Talk about kids.

   BERNADETTE *laughs bleakly.*

   Serious.

BERNADETTE. Now?!

OLIVER. If it's something we want...

BERNADETTE. We said not while

OLIVER. Thought it wasn't going away?

   Pause.

   Is it something we want?

   Pause. BERNADETTE*'s reeling. More bleak laughter.*

BERNADETTE. Yes. No. Painful, scary… Massive. Like, a *life*! Time off. Lose cases. Position. Salary maybe. Expensive – pencil cases. Kid grows in this? Speaks slowly. Maybe listens more? Bad for our… Struggling for words now. Miserable. But maybe joy? They say joy?

OLIVER. Done?

BERNADETTE. Almost.

OLIVER. Who'd be better?

BERNADETTE. Parent?

OLIVER. Yeah.

BERNADETTE looks at him, open-mouthed.

Joke!

Really.

Beat.

He looks at the floor.

(*Conciliatory.*) Maybe should start thinking like… this is world now.

BERNADETTE looks at him. Begins to let out a breath of relief.

*

OLIVER *is full of energy.*

BERNADETTE. Twenty-five.

OLIVER. Eight.

BERNADETTE. Think should book holiday.

OLIVER (*ignoring her*). Ohhhhhhhhh.

BERNADETTE. Greece or… Oh let's not fight about this. Parliament was on list.

OLIVER. Completely abusing it. Jesus.

BERNADETTE. Mmmm.

OLIVER. They're moving in.

BERNADETTE. You seem excited.

> OLIVER *holds his index finger up as if telling*
> BERNADETTE *to wait.*

What?

You're waiting for…

Pause.

OLIVER. One hundred forty.

BERNADETTE. Here we go.

OLIVER. They're moving into the House of Commons, Bernadette. It's a live-in words sanctuary for the powerful. And know what they've got in there? Twenty-eight food outlets. Twenty-eight. In February they could eat at different one every day.

BERNADETTE. Not on leap years.

OLIVER. There's a parliamentary hairdresser, parliamentary florist, parliamentary gym complete with buffed-up parliamentary / personal trainers.

BERNADETTE. Words.

OLIVER. Don't care. That's why keeping press out. They've built cruise ship in middle of London, they're moving in and chatting.

BERNADETTE. Don't get it when people get excited about bad news.

OLIVER. This is what we needed.

BERNADETTE. The movement.

OLIVER. Everybody. Fuck the amendment, now we go full repeal.

BERNADETTE. Whoa, d'you think that's –

OLIVER. Need talk to Julie.

Pause.

BERNADETTE. Why did you and Julie break up?

OLIVER. This is big. Things could happen.

BERNADETTE (*mumbled*). Need be more honest with / each other.

OLIVER. They've fired first shot, thrown first brick.

BERNADETTE. Happy for you.

*

BERNADETTE. Good luck today.

OLIVER. I need to find my air horn.

BERNADETTE. Have you got your earplugs?

OLIVER. Yeah, I've got them but I'm not gonna / wear them.

BERNADETTE. Please wear them.

OLIVER. I want to hear it all.

BERNADETTE. The noise.

OLIVER. The noise.

Pause.

BERNADETTE. The vote's on Wednesday?

OLIVER. Yep.

BERNADETTE. Five days. Oliver, I'm sorry if you think…

OLIVER. You don't believe in it, Bernadette. I'm not asking / you to.

BERNADETTE. It's not that I don't believe in it. Really. I do believe in it. / It's a bad law.

OLIVER. It's that you don't feel it.

BERNADETTE. Well, I'm sorry if that's not enough / for me to just agree.

OLIVER. I'm sorry, I'm just trying to imagine not feeling the need to speak out against this. And I can't. And don't give me all that about it being a group of middle-class people who like the sound of their own voice. Maybe that's true of the organisers. *Maybe*. But there'll be people from all walks of life out there today.

BERNADETTE. I'm just – I don't have the level of certainty that you have. About anything. I'd love to have that but I don't. Is that so unforgivable?

OLIVER. Uh. I dunno. Maybe it is. When the stakes are this high, maybe sitting back and saying 'oh but it's complicated'… maybe that is unforgivable. Listen, I love you but if it passes and you have to explain to like, *our kids*, that you felt kinda awkward at the protests so didn't bother turning up… I don't know Bernadette, maybe that is unforgivable?

BERNADETTE. It's not gonna pass.

OLIVER. I really hope you're right.

BERNADETTE. Well I hope you feel like a fucking rock star today Oliver for once in your life.

Pause.

OLIVER. Screw the air horn, I'll just shout.

BERNADETTE. Good luck.

OLIVER. Thanks.

*

OLIVER. Six.

BERNADETTE. Twenty-four.

OLIVER. Busy Friday.

BERNADETTE. Dinner with Mum.

OLIVER. You…

BERNADETTE. I go alone?

He nods.

What's going on?

OLIVER. Big fundraiser Friday.

He runs out of words.

BERNADETTE. Ahead of anniversary?

OLIVER *nods.*

Coming with this time.

Pause. OLIVER *looks uncertain.*

Coming with you.

*

OLIVER. One hundred six.

BERNADETTE. One hundred twelve.

They smile at each other. Silence.

OLIVER. Beautiful.

BERNADETTE. I look?

OLIVER. Yeah.

Pause.

BERNADETTE. Thanks.

*

BERNADETTE. Neville's a prick.

OLIVER. He's funny. Big name.

BERNADETTE. Kept putting his hands on me.

OLIVER. Being friendly.

BERNADETTE. He's a slimy slimeball of a man.

OLIVER. Words. And he's my friend.

BERNADETTE. Wish he wasn't.

  You were with her all night.

OLIVER. Who?

BERNADETTE. Your 'vandal'.

OLIVER. Just grow a backbone, Bernadette.

BERNADETTE. Sorry?

OLIVER. I said just grow a fucking

  OLIVER *attempts to say backbone but no sound comes out.*

BERNADETTE. Are you out?

  OLIVER *paces in frustration.*

You're out. Well I've got loads left, Oliver. I saved my words for you, Oliver. I've got words to throw away because nobody even spoke to me at your angry freedom party.

Silence.

Deserts.

Pause. OLIVER *looks at her confused.*

Buffalo. Holidays. Pasties. Aliens. Terrorism. Creep. Wasted. California. Rhinoceros. Lemons.

Pause.

Lemons. Lemons. Lemons. Lemons. Lemons. Done.

Long silence.

                        *

BERNADETTE. Sixteen.

OLIVER. Six.

BERNADETTE. Pass the salt.

  Pause.

Why did you and Julie break up?

Pause.

You're running low.

OLIVER. She didn't really love me any more.

Pause.

BERNADETTE. Pass the gravy.

*

OLIVER. Thirty-two.

BERNADETTE. Twelve.

*

OLIVER. Twenty-seven.

BERNADETTE. Five.

*

OLIVER. Forty.

BERNADETTE. Fourteen.

*

OLIVER. One hundred three.

BERNADETTE. Seven.

OLIVER. WHAT ARE YOU THINKING?

*

OLIVER. Six.

BERNADETTE. Three.

*

OLIVER. Four.

BERNADETTE. Eight.

*

OLIVER. Two.

BERNADETTE *does not respond.*

Zero?

She nods.

Right.

*

OLIVER. Hi. Don't.

BERNADETTE *stops herself.*

Pause.

Let's just talk until it goes. Without trying to...

BERNADETTE. Okay.

OLIVER. I miss you.

BERNADETTE. I'm here.

Pause.

OLIVER. It feels like we've both been pretending that you're not.

BERNADETTE *smiles slightly.*

BERNADETTE. That's exactly how it feels.

Pause.

OLIVER. Okay.

BERNADETTE. I'm running low.

OLIVER. Okay.

BERNADETTE. I'm sorry for...

OLIVER. Me too.

Pause. OLIVER *lowers himself to the floor.*

BERNADETTE *follows suit.*

After a moment.

BERNADETTE. Is it now?

She runs out of words.

OLIVER. Is it now?

Pause. He realises what she means.

Are you asking or telling?

BERNADETTE *thinks then shrugs, shakes her head: 'I don't know.'*

I don't have to go to anniversary march.

Can skip it.

If that...

BERNADETTE *shrugs.*

Pause.

BERNADETTE *taps the floor three times.*

S.

OLIVER *taps the floor three times.*

BERNADETTE *copies.*

OLIVER *taps the floor three times with his right hand and once with his left.*

BERNADETTE *copies.*

Eventually OLIVER *begins to tap out a rhythm on the floor.*

BERNADETTE *begins to drum with him.*

This continues for a few moments.

Then they fall silent.

Not now. Not yet.

*

BERNADETTE. Twenty-five.

OLIVER. Twenty-two.

BERNADETTE. Haircut! Love.

OLIVER. Work?

   BERNADETTE *groans*.

BERNADETTE. Liv won't sign.

OLIVER. Second weekend?

BERNADETTE. Yep. Shooting foot.

OLIVER. Donna all over again. Feel?

BERNADETTE. Seething.

   They laugh.

   Day?

OLIVER. Good! Progress horns.

BERNADETTE. Show?

   OLIVER *looks uneasy*.

   As when. C'wait t'listen.

OLIVER. Oh! Dan's Wednesday.

BERNADETTE. Keen?

OLIVER. Yeah.

BERNADETTE. Meet by place with red

OLIVER....Red?

BERNADETTE. The

OLIVER. Oh! Yes! The – yes!

                    *

OLIVER. Five.

BERNADETTE. Two.

   Pause.

OLIVER. I sometimes believe in God.

Pause. She looks at him, shaking her head. This is new information to her.

After a moment:

BERNADETTE. I'd wondered.

They smile at each other softly.

*

OLIVER. Nine.

BERNADETTE. Eight.

OLIVER. Squids.

BERNADETTE. Ink.

OLIVER. Poems.

BERNADETTE. Haikus.

OLIVER. Nagasaki.

BERNADETTE. Bombs?

OLIVER. Sex.

BERNADETTE. Shower.

OLIVER. Sex.

BERNADETTE. Now?

Beat.

OLIVER. Finish.

'Finish.'

BERNADETTE. Uh… beginning?

OLIVER. Cemetery.

BERNADETTE. Pets.

OLIVER. Embarrassing.

BERNADETTE. Young.

*

OLIVER. Kids playing in square.

BERNADETTE. Football. Dancing to busker.

OLIVER. You wearing that blue billowy

BERNADETTE. No, bought after

OLIVER. Swear

BERNADETTE. Bought for leaving do. Following June.

OLIVER. Drinking?

BERNADETTE. Sangria?

OLIVER. Hate sangria.

BERNADETTE. Oh yeah. But something in jug

OLIVER. Really?

BERNADETTE. Yes, cos noticed first raindrops in

OLIVER. We'd had argument night before

BERNADETTE. No!

OLIVER. Always on phone.

BERNADETTE. That was France.

OLIVER. Was it? What had –

BERNADETTE. We'd... walked the

OLIVER. What?

BERNADETTE. ...Not worth describing...

Beat.

OLIVER. That's when / the barman

BERNADETTE. Rain started

OLIVER. No, what?

BERNADETTE. Rain shower pouring

OLIVER. No, way later. Funny bit was barman screaming in

BERNADETTE (*struggling to remember*). Oh! Yes! Screaming what?

> OLIVER *sighs*. *He's almost out of words.*

OLIVER. That...

BERNADETTE. Sorry... (*i.e. the memory.*) it's like, *right* there...

> *Beat.*

> I'll remember. I will.

> It's not gone.

                                        *

OLIVER. Fifty-three

BERNADETTE. Thirty.

OLIVER. Where been?

BERNADETTE. Sorry, needed walk.

OLIVER. Came to court today. T'watch.

BERNADETTE. Oh. Family courts are closed...

OLIVER. I'd forgotten.

BERNADETTE. Sweet that you came.

> *Beat.* BERNADETTE *busies herself.*

OLIVER. Stood near door. Could um... could hear you. Sorf. Muffled...

> *She turns round.*

> Caught your closing statement.

BERNADETTE. Oh.

OLIVER. It was long!

BERNADETTE. Yeah. I –

OLIVER. Hearing your voice. You speaking so

Was…

Just closed my eyes for a while.

Listened.

Didn't matter that I couldn't really make out what you were

Just hearing

Felt like you were, I dunno

Stepping into the light.

Pause.

BERNADETTE. We lost.

OLIVER. Oh. I'm sorry.

BERNADETTE. I… wrong tack.

OLIVER. Sorry.

Beat.

BERNADETTE. Sweet that you… You're trying.

OLIVER. Yeah.

BERNADETTE. But it does matter what I was saying.

*

OLIVER. Ninety-four.

BERNADETTE. Forty-seven. So?

OLIVER. I am gonna go.

BERNADETTE. To the march.

OLIVER. I need to.

BERNADETTE. Why?

OLIVER. Not about me.

BERNADETTE. Okay.

OLIVER. Bernadette.

BERNADETTE. Yeah?

OLIVER. Before it was.

BERNADETTE. About you.

OLIVER. Yeah.

BERNADETTE. You were scared.

OLIVER. Insecure.

Pause.

BERNADETTE. It's an unjust law.

OLIVER. And now that's all it is.

Pause.

BERNADETTE. I'm coming with.

OLIVER. Babysitting again.

BERNADETTE. No. For you.

OLIVER. Lawyer on a protest march.

BERNADETTE. Oliver.

OLIVER. Family lawyer.

BERNADETTE. I work at a law firm. During some hours.

OLIVER. And now that's all it is?

BERNADETTE. It can be both. Many.

Pause.

Nothing's gonna change.

OLIVER *smiles sadly and nods.*

OLIVER. I know.

*

They breathe deeply.

BERNADETTE. Whoa.

OLIVER. Yeah, that's…?

BERNADETTE. Yeah.

   Pause.

   Ah.

OLIVER. Sorry.

BERNADETTE. No. Good.

OLIVER. Running low.

BERNADETTE. Really good.

                        *

OLIVER. Hundred thirty-seven.

BERNADETTE. Hundred thirty-six. What want do today?

OLIVER. Just get it all out?

BERNADETTE. Get it all out?

   OLIVER *begins to sing a song.*

   BERNADETTE *joins in.*

   OLIVER *sings until he runs out of words.*

   BERNADETTE *continues alone until she too runs out of
   words which happens long before the song's end.*

   Silence.

                        *

They look at each other a moment. Softly:

BERNADETTE. Forty-three.

OLIVER. Forty-three.

   They note the unlikeliness.

   Silence.

They look at each other. Something is happening.

BERNADETTE. Is it now?

Pause.

OLIVER. 'is it now'

He shakes his head as if saying 'I have no idea' to himself.

Beat.

BERNADETTE. Don't want. But

OLIVER. Talk.

BERNADETTE. Conversation.

OLIVER. Yeah.

Pause.

Lovou.

BERNADETTE. Lovou.

OLIVER. Really.

Pause.

Feel completely different to who I

BERNADETTE. Me too.

OLIVER. In good way.

BERNADETTE. Me too.

Beat.

OLIVER. Wish

Could express

How

BERNADETTE. I know it.

OLIVER. Magnificent.

Pause.

BERNADETTE. Before I... We...

Everything... contained.

Then...

Like door, thrown open.

Beat.

Think you make, always made, my world feel bigger.

But sometimes, make me feel smaller in it.

Beat.

OLIVER. Never thought.

BERNADETTE. Sometimes.

Pause.

OLIVER. Need to tell you something.

Pause.

BERNADETTE. Okay.

Beat.

OLIVER. On day of the noise march...

BERNADETTE. Space noise march.

OLIVER. Yeah.

BERNADETTE. When you and Julie threw the...

Pause.

OLIVER. I slept with her.

Pause.

BERNADETTE. I think I knew.

OLIVER. I think I knew you knew.

Long pause.

BERNADETTE. Thanks for telling me though.

*

BERNADETTE. Instead of 'I love you' we could say 'lovou'.

OLIVER. Yes. Definitely. Exactly.

BERNADETTE. Great.

OLIVER. Great.

BERNADETTE. I think we're going to deal with this really well.

OLIVER. Yeah, I think we'll be completely fine.

BERNADETTE. Really / fine.

OLIVER. Really fine. And if, I mean if we ever don't quite understand each other, what the other / is trying to

BERNADETTE. I think we will though.

OLIVER. Yeah I know we definitely will. Because we're so well / prepared.

BERNADETTE. Well prepared. / Exactly.

OLIVER. But if we don't. I mean if the time ever comes where we don't quite get...

BERNADETTE. Right.

OLIVER. We could say 'dunderstand'.

BERNADETTE. 'Dunderstand.'

OLIVER. Yeah.

BERNADETTE. That's a good one.

OLIVER. Thanks.

BERNADETTE. I suppose it's about finding little tricks like you said.

OLIVER. Yes. I think so. Sort of.

BERNADETTE. Sorf.

OLIVER. Sorf.

Pause. They smile.

BERNADETTE. Let's just keep it / in the

OLIVER. Back of our heads.

BERNADETTE. Exactly.

We've got time.

End of play.

www.nickhernbooks.co.uk

facebook.com/nickhernbooks

twitter.com/nickhernbooks